Many thanks go to Michelle, Sara and Danica. Without the wonderful and insightful Ladies of Lunae, this book would never have existed.

Contents

Preface

Lunae is a tradition of Wicca that was born from the way I was raised and the life that I live. One of the hats that I wear is that of High Priestess to a coven of wonderful people, who have insisted for a while now that I have to write a book about my beliefs and practices. If I had a nickel for every time I've heard the phrase "That's going to be in the book, right?" I'd be a rich woman right about now.

Wicca is a religion of individuality and personal responsibility, unique and different for every person who lives it. My mother taught me that each person has their own individual pathway to the divine and it isn't up to me, or anyone else for that matter, to show them their path or where it will lead. My job, my responsibility, in this life is simply to teach them how to walk, maybe interpret a few signposts until they learn the language, and help them find the tools that they'll need along the way. Once they start walking, the journey is their own.

So, yes, this may be just another book about Wicca. It might, however, help a few people to better understand the specifics of Lunae Wicca. I'm not an expert on anything. I'm simply a woman who has experienced life in a way that most others of my generation have not and I've been asked to share that. Since I don't have any children of my own to pass anything down to, writing a book seemed like a good way to share what I believe with those who are interested in hearing about it.

This book is also a collaborative effort with the women of my coven. We integrated my family's teachings and those of Wicca, in writing, in order to have a cohesive and comprehensive teaching tool for the present and future students of our school, the Lunae Institute of Metaphysical and Religious Studies, otherwise known as LIMRS (pronounced lē-murs). Much of what is written here is presented in first person format simply because it is easier for me to write it that way, but there are many people speaking behind the "I" that is doing the actual typing.

Erianne Eads, HPS, M.Div., RM
Jera Kenaz Lunae Coven

Introduction

History

I choose to begin my history of Wicca and the Witch, not in the past, but in the present. My reason is simply that the history of the Witch is the history of mankind. Witchcraft existed prior to the recognizing of formal religion and, in my opinion, is the force behind the creation of all religious groups. There is also the small matter of the commonly accepted adage that not all Wiccans are Witches, just as not all Witches are Wiccan.

Many modern day Wiccans choose to immerse themselves in the religious aspect of Wicca, preferring to work only within the practice of spirituality rather than with the powers of magic necessary to perform spell and energy work. Conversely, there are those that make such magical workings a high priority within their individual or group practice of the religion. I suspect, however, that the majority of currently practicing Wiccans fall within the middle ground, striving continually for a perfect harmony and balance between the two.

Where does Wicca come from? For this, we must turn first to the ancient past. The specific origins of modern day Wicca are widely disputed, but one has only to look upon the 30,000-year-old cave drawings in France to understand that the roots of Wicca run deep. The drawings depict 11 humans standing in a circle with their hunter god, shown as a man's body bearing the head of a horned stag, and their fertility goddess, a woman with a very swollen, obviously pregnant belly. Even Paleolithic man recognized the need to honor those forces of nature that allowed him to survive and fostered his continued lineage. He appreciated that there were other powers at work in his life, beyond his limited concept of self, beings that were the same yet different than mankind at a base level. His concept of deity was struggling to be born.

It was a natural progression from this infantile view of God and Goddess to the stepping forward of those with a claim of greater connection and inborn understanding. Every culture has either a written or verbal tradition depicting the stories of these individuals. They were the shaman, the healers, the sages, the village wise women, those who walked with one foot in the land of man and the other in the land of the gods. These shamans were revered and held in great awe for their ability to summon spirits, beings and forces beyond the understanding of the common tribesmen. In the beginning, they were treated as if they were the embodiment of the powers they used.

Eventually, those around them began to understand that the real power lay within the beings called upon, not particularly within those who were delivering the demonstrations of that power to the common people. They began to worship, not the wielders of the power, but the power itself. They gave the beings names, attributed various faces and abilities to each and the shamans were then thought to be only the representatives of these gods, not the gods themselves. Thus base religion was born into the world of man.

Rituals and ceremonies were created in honor of and to please their deities. Drawings were made before a hunt to show the gods what they desired, gifts were given in exchange for the requested bounty, dances were performed and songs offered up for the pleasure of the gods in the belief that a happy god was a giving one. Rituals were changed and adapted to account for the various needs that occurred in their daily lives. Rites of passage were developed to mark the milestones of life. When disasters struck, special ceremonies were held to offer appeasement for the assumed anger of their gods. There are records of such occurrences throughout history from virtually every culture around the world. Religion, though growing more prevalent, was still in its infancy.

What has this to do with modern Wicca? This is the beginning of all religion, thus the ancient beginning of Wicca itself. In 1939, "Old Dorothy" Clutterback initiated Gerald Gardner into a coven of witches in the New Forest area of Britain that practiced the "Old Religion". Where did that coven come from and what was the "Old Religion"? They were the end result of these beginnings, after man had spread across the globe, adapted his beliefs to his environment, and expanded his knowledge and understanding of both the forces of nature and of his gods. Thus, the coven and religion into which Gardner was initiated were but the adolescent stage of primitive man's belief in a power outside of himself.

Gerald Gardner drew both knowledge and inspiration for the creation of Wicca from many sources. Not only from the teachings of the New Forest Witches, but also from the OTO (Ordo Templi Orientis – the Order of Oriental Templars), the Hermetic Order of the Golden Dawn, the Rosicrucian Society, and especially the Freemasons. Gardner always claimed that the rituals that he had received from his coven were very sparse; therefore, he combined them with a mixture of ceremonial magic and Freemasonry to form the basis of Wicca as we know it today.

Let's look briefly at those groups from which he garnered his knowledge and foundation for the creation of Wicca. The Hermetic Order of the Golden Dawn was founded in 1888, bringing about a renewed societal interest in the occult. They made available rituals and a large body of occult lore that would have remained hidden and inaccessible otherwise. This Order was itself a descendant of the esoteric traditions of Rosicrucianism, Theosophy and Freemasonry.

The Rosicrucian Society was founded in 1408 by a German nobleman. It is considered by some to be a spin-off Order of the Knights Templar and venerates the rose and the cross as the symbols of Christ's redemption and resurrection. They are known to practice a unique combination of mysticism, alchemy and the occult.

Theosophy, literally meaning "god-wisdom", is a doctrine which combines metaphysics and religious philosophy, founded in 1875 in New York City by Madame Helena P. Blavatsky. Members believe that all religions are attempts by the "Occult Brotherhood" (adepts or Mahatmas) to help humanity evolve to a greater perfection and that each individual religion is but a part of the greater whole.

The Order of Oriental Templars, also known as Ordo Templi Orientis (OTO), is thought to have been founded in Germany or Austria in 1895 by Carl Kellner. It was intended to be modeled after Freemasonry, but under the leadership of Aleister Crowley, it was restructured and reorganized around the Law of Thelema, which is "Do what thou wilt shall be the whole of the Law" and "Love is the law, love under will". The ecclesiastical branch of OTO is the Gnostic Catholic Church, whose public central rite is the Gnostic Mass.

Aleister Crowley was initiated into the Hermetic Order of the Golden Dawn in 1898, and in 1903 he founded his own Order, the Argentum Astrum or Silver Star. In 1912, Crowley was initiated into the OTO and became its Chief in 1921. In 1946, Crowley gave Gardner an OTO charter, after which he began to introduce material from the OTO and the Order of the Golden Dawn into his covens.

As Crowley and Gardner were both Masons, it is not surprising that one encounters structural similarities between Freemasonry and Wicca, which include use of the following:

> A three-tiered degree system
> The name "The Craft"
> Use of the phrase "So mote it be"
> Presentation of working tools upon attaining First Degree

In 1951, England repealed the last of its remaining laws against witchcraft. Gardner, who had continued to practice in secret with the New Forest coven, now felt able to break free of them, go public and establish his own group. In 1953, Gardner met Doreen Valiente and initiated her into his coven. In collaboration, they rewrote and expanded Gardner's existing texts and rituals. She also removed much of the works and embellishments by Aleister Crowley, inserted the influences of Charles Leland, an authority on gypsies and Italian witchcraft, and began to bring more emphasis on goddess worship. The most widely known example of this is "The Charge of the Goddess". Together, they created the working practice that eventually evolved into what is known today as the Gardnerian tradition. Valiente, in time, became the High Priestess of Gardner's coven.

In 1957, a chasm developed between Gardner and the coven over his insertion of laws insinuating the dominance of God over Goddess. Doreen Valiente left to form her own coven within the Gardnerian tradition, later abandoning the tradition to become an initiate in the "1734" tradition, founded by self-labeled hereditary witch, Robert Cochrane.

On June 6, 1960, Gardner initiated Patricia Dawson, who in turn initiated Arnold Crowther. Dawson and Crowther were subsequently married, moved to Sheffield, England, and used media publicity to spread the word about witchcraft. They went on to start many new covens throughout the country.

In 1963, Gardner met Raymond Buckland in Perth, Scotland, at the home of his then High Priestess, Monique Wilson. Monique Wilson initiated Buckland, who then carried the Gardnerian tradition to the United States in 1964. Also in the 1960's, Alex Sanders attempted to gain entrance to several Gardnerian covens, but was consistently refused admittance. He obtained a copy of Gardner's Book of Shadows, which he then copied and embellished, adding his own amendments, which he subsequently claimed as a copy of his own grandmother's Book of Shadows. He used this as the basis for forming his own coven, practicing what was later to be known as the Alexandrian tradition. In 1968, while appearing in a film called "Legend of the Witches", he was introduced to Stewart Farrar, whom many consider, along with wife, Janet, to be the originator of the "eclectic" tradition of Wicca.

In 1973, in the United States, Raymond Buckland decided to leave the Gardnerian tradition, feeling it no longer met his religious needs and was filled with extreme egotism and politics. He founded the tradition of Seax-Wica, which was based on a Saxon heritage and was more open and democratic.

From these beginnings comes the diversity of traditions that comprise modern Wicca. It is said that there are as many different traditions of Wicca as there are Wiccans. I believe this to be an accurate view. No two people think, act, communicate, worship, or believe alike. Therefore, it's logical to assume that there will be no two Wiccans who practice their religion exactly the same. Each path is as unique as they who walk it. That's the beauty of this religion.

1

Lunae

In many ways, I had a very unorthodox upbringing. My parents were essentially pagan and believed that each individual's pathway to the divine was personal; that the divine energies in this universe are the same, no matter what name you use to address them or what gender you are more comfortable envisioning them as; that all religions are valid for those who walk them in true faith and belief; that no one religion has all of the answers; that all religious paths deserve respect and are beautiful in their own right; and that no one has the right to judge or condemn the path of any other.

Add to that the teachings of my grandmother, who was a Christian by choice, yet taught me about the lunar and solar celebrations of Wicca. She also taught me about spell work and magic, the energies of the elements, how to hex and heal, everything that had been passed to her by her "hill folk" ancestors. She called it "granny magic". My grandmother bore 16 children and there are a myriad of faiths practiced by my aunts, uncles, cousins, and within my own immediate family as well. Many different sects of Christianity are represented, as well as Catholicism, several pagan paths, Theosophists, Gnostics, Agnostics, and even an atheist thrown in there for good measure.

This led to a very well-rounded childhood for me personally, spiritually speaking. I studied many of the "mainstream" religions, as well as a great many of those that were not so well known. Plainly stated, I love religion, all religion. I think that working towards a better understanding of, and closer relationship with, the divine is a beautiful and transformative journey that makes your heart smile and your soul sing.

My father says that life is a school and that it's up to you to get the best education you can while you're here. I've spent my life trying to do just that. Now I try to help others maximize their own potential and garner all the beauty, knowledge and understanding that they possibly can from this school before the bell rings and class is over for this particular lifetime.

So what does it mean to be Lunae? As I said in the introduction, the Lunae tradition is an eclectic path of Wicca combined with the spiritual beliefs and magical practices that were taught to me by my parents and maternal grandmother. Lunae students, both those who are taught individually and those who attend classes via LIMRS, learn about the meaning behind both the coven and tradition names. They are expected to learn about each of the elements and work with their respective energies, including deity.

They receive traduism-specific training in many areas, such as:

Sabbat traditions and beliefs

Esbats

Ritual form, steps, and etiquette

Degree system and hierarchy

Focus of the tradition

Official symbols *(which differ slightly from that of other traditions)*

Meanings behind those symbols

Wiccan Rede *(long version by Doreen Valiente)*

Pagan citizenship

Ethics

Energy and spell work

This is just a small sampling of the type of training that our students must be prepared for when they board this particular educational train. It isn't easy, nor should it be, but it is as thorough and rewarding as we can make it.

We are a family-oriented tradition. This is a large part of who we are and what we do. Just as several generations of my family taught me, I consider it both a privilege and a responsibility to pass those teachings on to future generations. I began teaching religion, philosophy and magic to my stepdaughter and oldest nephew when they were 2 and 3 years old. They learned about paganism in general and Wicca specifically, but they also learned about Christianity, Hinduism, and Catholicism (both of their fathers are Catholic). They were both equally eager students and the lessons progressed as they aged.

During their early teen years, each made their own choices about where the path was leading them. My stepdaughter chose Catholicism as her spiritual home and I fully supported her in that. My nephew decided to study Wicca a little further by working with the coven I was training in at the time. He eventually went his own direction and has not participated in ritual with me for a few years now. His mother (my sister) played an integral role in the creation of Jera Kenaz Lunae's astral temple and was an active participant in several of our early rituals. Another sister fills the important role of visiting teacher and hedge witching resource for our coven. My youngest sister is pagan clergy and devotes much time and energy to healing and counseling others.

We continue this tradition by including our members' children in rituals, classes, community service and other activities at levels consistent with their ages and understanding of what is being done.

2

Beliefs and Focus

Let's begin with the direction in which the Lunae tradition is focused.

We strive toward personal and group balance in all things: male and female; positive and negative; physical and spiritual; mundane and magical; and God and Goddess. Therefore:

1. We believe in developing a balanced working relationship with the elements. Our tradition teaches that only a balance of the elemental energies of Air, Fire, Earth and Water, under the guidance of Spirit, will create and maintain a magical, spiritual and fulfilling incarnation.

2. We believe that neither male nor female energy is dominant over the other and that a balanced respect for and working relationship with both God and Goddess is vital to our wholeness.

3. We believe that universal order can only be maintained through a balance of positive and negative energies. We teach from the philosophy that those who cannot hex lack the ability to heal, meaning that those who cannot affect the universe negatively will lack the power and ability to affect positive change.

We stress the importance of ongoing education, community service, and personal growth. Without continued growth and learning, there can be no evolution on either the physical or spiritual level. Community service and public education are also vital components to ensure and further this evolution.

Our coven name is Jera Kenaz Lunae, which means:

Jera	=	Harvest
Kenaz	=	Torch
Lunae	=	Moons

The coven name demonstrates our recognition of the phases through which all things must flow and honors those who designed and lead us through these phases.

Jera represents the cycles of life, death and rebirth. We are the seeds that have been sown by deity to grow and die, only to be replanted and grow yet again. We are the harvest of the gods.

Kenaz is the torch within, the spark of deity that fuels us, enlightening the darkness of the voids.

Lunae represents the balance and unity of God and Goddess. The moon is associated with Goddess, the dark night and hidden things, including our own inner selves. The visual phases that we observe – waxing, full, waning and dark – typify the phases that we must pass through during our physical lives.

The sun is associated with God, the bright day and all that is easily seen, including our outer selves. Without the light of the sun, we would be unable to see the moon and it is this outer light that balances and illuminates the inner darkness.

As I stated previously, the pentacle that our tradition uses differs slightly from those of other Wiccan traditions and pagan paths. Here is our pentacle and the reasoning behind its differences.

A pentacle is a five-pointed star surrounded by a circle whose points represent the five elements, the circle enclosing them representing the whole or the world. The pentacle symbolizes that it takes all the elements together to make the whole work correctly – whether that is the world, the universe or our bodies. The Lunae tradition pentacle and an explanation of how we view it:

Both male and female are represented on each half, whether it's the top and bottom or left and right. This demonstrates an absolute balance governed overall by Spirit.

When looking at the surrounding elements:

Water and Earth can both control Fire. Water douses and Earth smothers Fire.

Air and Fire can both control Earth. Fire burns its growth off and Air erodes the soil or whips up sandstorms.

Water and Earth can control Air. Large volumes of Water can slow it down or change its movements and Earth can block it with hills, mountains or trees.

Fire and Air can control Water. Fire can evaporate it and Air can suck it up and carry it away.

Spirit is at the top because it is the force that keeps the others balanced and in check. It is the set of natural laws that govern the universe.

Lunae students that are working within JKL (Jera Kenaz Lunae) coven are assigned a mentor and given three booklets: Dedicant Guide, Degree System, and Coven Bylaws. This allows them to see upfront what is expected of them, as well as what they may expect from us. Their mentor is provided with an additional booklet, the Mentorship Guide, which outlines quite plainly what both the coven and tradition expect from them as a guide and mentor.

One of the first things a student must learn is the hierarchy, which is based upon the levels of the degree system.

Dedicant – this is someone who has chosen to make a formal commitment to study Wicca for a year and a day. They are given a white cord, worn around the waist, to designate their standing. Dedicants may apply to work as a student of the coven. The High Council is responsible for accepting or rejecting such applications.

Initiate – this is a Dedicant who has completed their year and a day, has declared Wicca as their chosen spiritual and religious path, and are initiated into Wicca by the High Priestess. They are recognized as a priest or priestess of Wicca at this time and are given a yellow cord to symbolize completion of their Air year. Initiates may apply to become a full member of the coven. A unanimous decision by all full voting members is required to approve such applications.

First Degree – this is a coven member who has completed their year and a day at the Initiate level, having completed all the necessary requirements as outlined in the coven degree system. They are now recognized by the coven as a practicing witch and are given a red cord to signify completion of their Fire year.

Second Degree – this is a coven member who has completed their year and a day, as well as the degree system requirements, at the First Degree level. They are initiated as a member of the Lunae tradition clergy and receive a blue cord to signify completion of their Water year.

Third Degree – this is a coven member who has completed their year and a day, as well as the degree system requirements, at the Second Degree level. They are given a green cord to symbolize completion of their Earth year.

Elder – to petition for Elder status, the person must have completed their year and a day at the Third Degree level, as well as the degree system requirements, and have been a coven member in good standing for a minimum of five years. If approved and initiated, they are given a purple cord to symbolize completion of their Spirit year.

High Priest/Priestess – any coven member who has attained Elder status may petition to be initiated as a High Priest or High Priestess after completing the additional degree system requirements. If approved and initiated, they are given a black cord to symbolize completion of the degree system and may apply for a charter to hive off and start their own coven within the Lunae tradition.

The remaining chapters present information on many of the topics that all beginning Lunae students are expected to study during their Dedicant year.

3

Deity

Ancient man looked up at the moon in awe and worshipped it. In order to give it proper honor, the moon was given a human face and name in order to be able to bring a piece of it to earth in the form of statues, paintings, writings, etc. They then decided that since the moon was so bright in the sky that it must be in charge of the night when all else is dark. When they needed strength in the dark, they would look to the moon and call its earthly name to guide them and lead them through their darkness.

This is how all the names of the gods began. People would have a need and want a higher power to look to for guidance, so they gave a name and face to the side of God or Goddess that they believed was in control of that particular thing they needed. This is one of the reasons that Spirit has so many different faces and names around the world.

There are no gods and goddesses that are strictly Wiccan. In the Lunae tradition of Wicca, we believe that there is one Universal Spirit or guiding light in the universe that has both a male and female aspect.

We, as humans, give this divine energy whatever names and faces that we feel necessary in an attempt to comprehend the many facets of deity and the divine. Wiccans call upon the gods and goddesses by any or all of their names, using whichever names represent the aspects that they need at that moment. Lunae belief is that Zeus, Apollo, Loki, Yahweh, Allah, Vishnu, etc. are all the same deity – the universal male spirit. Only the names, mythology, duties, and methods of worship differ. An example is given in the illustration below.

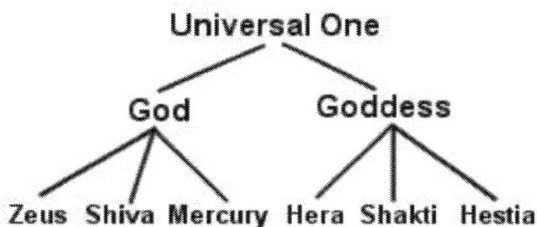

Universal One

God   **Goddess**

Zeus Shiva Mercury   Hera Shakti Hestia

Wicca celebrates both God and Goddess in triple aspect. For Goddess this is known as Maiden, Mother and Crone, for God it is Youth, Father and Sage. These aspects represent not only the physical aging that we go through in the normal course of our lives, but the psychological and emotional changes as well. During the Maiden/Youth phase, deity is seen as exhibiting youthful attributes such as being lighthearted and carefree, much as we act during our childhoods. This can also include the bravado and foolishness often seen during the teenage years. Even in indigenous populations, few responsibilities are given to the young.

It is during the Mother/Father phase that deity is seen as taking on more responsibility and maturity. The Mother becomes more nurturing and guiding, the Father more protective and focused on providing. This is mirrored in the human adult phase as well – having children, creating a home, and building a career and financial stability. For indigenous peoples, there are often challenges to be overcome and rites that must be performed before one can be seen as an adult. By proving themselves worthy, they may take on mates, raise families, become hunters and gatherers, and join the world of mature tribal society.

The Crone/Sage phase is one of vast wisdom born from years of learning and experience. They are the leaders, teachers and healers that spend their time passing on their life lessons and accomplishments to the young. In tribal societies, these are the elders, chiefs and shamans. Sadly, the modern world makes little use of this important resource today, and I believe that we may eventually find that we're paying a high price for ignoring the wisdom of our elders.

There are also both light and dark attributes for each of these aspects. Nurturing, part of the Mother aspect, is a positive or "light" attribute. Carried to excess, it can become smothering or overbearing, which would be a negative or "dark" aspect.

We often don't call upon a specific deity. We invite and address deity as Great Mother and Great Father, Lord and Lady, or simply God and Goddess, because those are comforting and welcoming titles that demonstrate our honor and respect for them, inviting them to join us in whatever fashion they choose.

However, when doing a very specific working, like raising healing energy, we may choose to call specifically, for example, on Apollo because he is one of the gods of medicine and healing arts. For the goddess, we might call upon Airmid, a Celtic goddess of herbal knowledge and also a healer. When we have a specific need, we may then use a specific name of deity which is known, through myth and legend, to be associated with that type of energy.

In talking about and working with the energy of God and Goddess, we need to remember some very important information.

- the energy of deity is contained in all things, including us
- there is a dark and a light side to all things, including deity
- it is we who decide how to interact with these energies

Many mainstream religions teach that deity is "out there", outside of and just beyond our grasp. Lunae Wicca teaches that this is not the case. All energy comes from the Universal One. We are created from and share the same origin as all things in the universe. Scientists refer to the birth of our universe as "The Big Bang". Many pagan religions refer to it as "the Awakening". No matter what name you give it or mythology you assign, it's all the same – the birth moment of the universe – the moment in time when the consciousness of the Universal One began. It is from this that all other things come. Perhaps the "Big Bang" was simply the moment that the Universal One exploded itself outward in order to form all dimensions and planes of existence.

A great many people believe in the concept of a conscience, but few are willing to explore just exactly what that means. If you stop someone on the street and ask them what a conscience is, chances are they'll answer that it's the little voice inside that tells you whether something is right or wrong. How many people bother to wonder whose little voice is speaking? It surely isn't your own voice because, if you knew something was right or wrong, you wouldn't have to "tell" yourself. You would just do that thing based on what you know. That internal voice is deity, answering because you've asked the question – is this action right or wrong?

Yes, God and Goddess are "out there". What we need to remember, however, is that they are also "in here". We need look no further than ourselves to find them. It is just as effective to speak to them out loud as it is to whisper to them quietly within our hearts and minds. This isn't because of some mystical concept of a god who lives outside of us yet listens in on our every thought in order to judge us. It is simply because we carry their energy inside of us and have only to focus on it to make ourselves heard.

4

Elements and Correspondences

Correspondences are which stones, herbs, colors, etc. can be used together to create a specific atmosphere or enhance a particular magical intent, based on individual association with particular elemental attributes or energies.

The five elements are: Air, Fire, Water, Earth, and Spirit. Here are the basics of what each is and does:

Air is associated with the direction of east and governs various things in our lives – communication, speech, education and learning, intelligence, creativity and imagination, as well as our intellectual and spiritual thoughts. The color used to represent Air is yellow. Air is our minds and our breath, the two things that bring us life and make us who we are. Someone who is too much in their thoughts is said to have their head in the clouds. Someone whose thoughts zip around or who can't think clearly is often referred to as an airhead.

Some other things associated with the element of Air are:

Astrological signs: Gemini, Libra, Aquarius
Tools: wand, incense

Earth is associated with the direction of north and governs our physical body and surroundings. It represents the things that can be physically touched, such as our possessions, our bodies, our homes, and money. It also represents the planet and all the creatures on it, such as animals, as well as the trees, dirt, rocks, and mountains. The element of Earth is what keeps us grounded in reality. It is the physical reality of life that keeps us tied to our bodies and to other people and things. It is our roots. Our physical selves can be visualized as a tree – we have roots, our history that has brought us to where we are now; we have the trunk of the tree, the part of us that we allow others to see and touch readily and is the main part of who we are right now; then we have the branches and leaves that are our thoughts and spirit, reaching upward and outward to learn and pull us toward the lights in our lives. The colors that represent Earth are green and brown.

Some other things associated with the element of Earth are:

Astrological signs: Taurus, Virgo, Capricorn
Tools: pentacle, salt

Fire is associated with the direction of south and governs passion, lust, ambition, career, and anger. It is our will and our drive – to grow, to move forward and upward. It is what fuels us to keep going, the inner spark of deity which burns within our hearts. It is represented by the color red. When angry, we say we are seeing red. Someone with too much passion is said to have a fiery personality.

Some other things associated with the element of Fire are:

Astrological signs: Aries, Leo, Sagittarius
Tools: athame, censer

Water is associated with the direction of west and governs our emotions, our depth of being. It is love, fear, joy, pain, understanding and empathy. Humans can have such a range of emotions, good and bad, because we are mostly water. It is represented by the color blue. A good visual to remember is that we humans are like the ocean when it comes to our emotions. We have a surface that we let others see easily and can be either calm or stormy. We have undercurrents just below the surface that can control what our surface shows. But we also have depth to us; a depth that, like the ocean, can be dark and treacherous or peaceful, quiet and serene. That's why people who have great control over their emotions are said to be deep.

Some other things associated with the element of Water are:

Astrological signs: Cancer, Scorpio, Pisces
Tools: chalice, cauldron

Spirit is associated with the directions of inward and outward and governs all that is spiritual in our lives, including deity. Without Spirit, we are lifeless and stagnant. It is represented by the color white because white light contains all other colors of light within it. It is our destiny, our fate, our sense of self and self-worth. It is what controls and combines the other elements to create the sum total of our inner selves and who we are as a person. It represents our soul. Someone who is wise beyond their years and contemplates the meaning of life is said to be very spiritual.

Some other things associated with the element of Spirit are:

Tools: deity symbols

When I want to visualize the elements as something tangible, I see yellow butterflies for Air, a bonfire for Fire, a waterfall for Water, a large tree for Earth and the night sky filled with millions of stars for Spirit.

Try to notice all the ways that each of the elements works both together and separately in your life. If you talk on the phone or computer, think about how Air is helping you communicate. If you get angry or passionate about something, think about Fire. If something touches your heart, think about Water. If you buy something or when you use your keys to open the door to your home, think about Earth. Spirit is the hardest to see in your every day, but it is the one that is with you the most. Think about those things that keep you going and you'll be thinking about Spirit.

5

Wheel of the Year

The wheel of the year is a representation of the physical yearly cycle of the earth as it revolves around the sun. If you drew a circle to represent the entire year, then drew eight equally spaced lines, going completely across that circle so that all lines intersect at the same spot in the center, you would have an image that looks a lot like a wagon wheel. This is why we call it the "Wheel of the Year".

Each point where one of these lines touches the outer circle represents a particular day in that year. They represent the longest and shortest days of the year, the days when the hours of night and day are roughly equal, as well as the midpoint between each of these. Each point on the circle commemorates a specific event in the progression of the seasons on this planet. In Wicca, we refer to the celebration of these markers as sabbats. Many religions and cultures throughout the world also celebrate or acknowledge these milestones throughout the year with a multitude of festivals, but we will deal only with the Lunae viewpoint on this.

What is a sabbat? Simply put, it is a solar celebration, the marking of a milestone in the solar cycle. We celebrate that the sun has reached a particular viewing point in the sky or that the earth has reached a specific point in its orbital relationship with the sun. We use the sabbats to mark the turning of the seasons, to keep track of our progress through the year, to mark the growing and resting times of the fields, and to honor the cycle of life, death and rebirth as seen in the lives of our deities.

Why is all this important? Whether we realize it or not, we use this information often in our lives, especially those who make their living from working the land. We can use the passing of the sabbats in many useful ways. We use the information to decide when it's time to plant various crops or to harvest them. We can use it to determine when it's time to pack away our warm weather clothing and start digging out those sweaters and coats, or when it's time to pack those cold weather clothes and drag out the shorts and tank tops. When does daylight savings time start and end? It begins on the Sunday prior to the spring equinox (Ostara) and ends on the first Sunday after Samhain. We can also use them to guide our internal clocks. Outdoor fields are not the only place we plant our crops.

In order to understand what that can mean for us, let us now look at the individual points on the wheel and discuss the significance of each. The dates listed are the 3-day period in which the Lunae tradition celebrates these events, as passed down to me by my grandmother. Traditionally, in our family, each sabbat celebration was three days long. The day before was for preparations such as cleaning, cooking and decorating. The day of the sabbat was the community celebration, with everyone from the village or town gathering at a central location for a rite, which was followed by a shared feast, games, music and dancing. The final day was for the family observance with traditional rituals, foods and activities shared only within our own family group.

Yule, December 20-22, is the first official celebration in the Wiccan year. It is also known as the time of Winter Solstice, the longest night of the year. From that day onward, until Summer Solstice, the hours of daylight begin to lengthen and the hours of darkness shorten. One of the symbols of the god is the sun, which is reborn in the sense that it's dominion over the darkness starts anew that day. Yule also represents the midway point of the cold weather season and is a time of rest and inner contemplation. Just as the fields rest and recuperate in the winter, so should we. The goddess has given birth to the newborn god and begins her time as the Crone. For 6 weeks, she remains in isolation and tends to the young god, raising him in the bounty of her hard-won wisdom.

Imbolc, January 31 – February 2, is roughly the midpoint between Yule and Ostara, and is the first official day of spring on the Wiccan calendar. This is the time when we celebrate the first stirrings of life deep within the ground and begin preparing our tools for the coming planting season. This is symbolized by the legend of a sleepy groundhog making his way out of his burrow for the first forage of the year. It is the time when the world and all those in it begin to move from their time of rest and look forward to the time of planting. The goddess has completed her rest and, rejuvenated and renewed, is once again seen in the world as the young Maiden. The god is now a fast-growing Youth entering puberty.

Ostara, March 20-22, is also known as the Vernal Equinox. All of the world awakes from its slumber and throws off the chill of winter. The hours of daylight and darkness are now equal. We bang on the trunks of the trees with sticks to wake them up and to get their sap flowing. We decorate all the trees in our yard with colorful pieces of ribbon in the hope that the returning birds might use them in their nest building. We begin to break up the soil and start growing our plants in greenhouses in preparation for the upcoming planting season. As the land becomes fertile, so does the goddess. She and the god mate. As the seeds in the earth germinate into plants, his seed of life begins to germinate within the womb of the goddess. Her tears of joy are seen in the spring rains.

Beltane, April 30-May 2, is the wedding of God and Goddess. The fields are now being actively planted and the pregnancy of the goddess becomes obvious. Having each proved their fertility to the other, they wed with a grand celebration. We dance and weave the Maypole to join in their joy. The staff of the Maypole represents the god, and the ribbons of white and red symbolize the purity, and subsequent loss, of the goddess' maiden status. The descending crown of flowers represents their triumphant union which has resulted in the pregnancy. She is now the Mother and he is the Father, the Greenman, representing the full bloom of the earth.

Litha, June 20-22, is also known as the time of Summer Solstice, the longest day of the year, after which the hours of daylight begin to shorten and the hours of darkness to lengthen until Yule. The sun is at its peak of strength and so is the god. Now he represents the ultimate peak of manhood. The goddess is well into her pregnancy and the crops in the fields grow strong and full along with her.

Lammas, July 31-August 2, is the celebration of the first harvest, the harvest of the grains. As the grain is cut from the fields, the adult god begins to weaken, but the child within the goddess is becoming strong and active. She laments the coming loss of her husband, but takes comfort in the knowledge that he will be reborn from her.

Mabon, September 20-22, is also known as the Autumnal Equinox. It is the second of the harvest festivals and is commonly known as the Wiccan Thanksgiving. The hours of light and dark are again in balance. We celebrate not only the harvest of the trees and vines, but our inner harvests of the seeds we planted at Ostara. To symbolize this, we celebrate and share with those in our community whose personal harvests may not be as full or blessed as our own. The god, entering the autumn of his own life, becomes the Sage. In his wisdom, he acknowledges the full cycle of the wheel and realizes that he will die to make way for new life. He prepares now for this. The goddess feels sorrow at the impending death of her husband, represented by the chill autumn winds, but also much joy in his coming rebirth from her womb, which we see in the colorful beauty of the changing leaves.

Samhain (which we pronounce as sahm-**hān**) is the night when the old year dies. It is celebrated October 31-November 2, including the day commonly known as Halloween or All Hallows' Eve. For us, Halloween is the equivalent of New Year's Eve. Our new year begins on November 1st. With the final harvest of the gourds and pods, the god dies and travels through the veil to Summerland, leading the way for those who have also passed from earthly life and await rebirth. This is the time when the Western Gate is opened for those individuals who died throughout the year. As the goddess both grieves his loss and prepares for the coming birth, she enters isolation and her grief brings the cold winds. The snowflakes are her tears, frozen by her grief.

The wheel of the year is an important tool that we use to represent, in a physical manner, all which is seen and unseen in the world, the ongoing cycle of life, death and rebirth to which all must subscribe. It is the earth's own calendar.

6

Esbats

The moon is associated with our emotions and symbolizes the hidden mysteries of life. It has both an emotional and physical effect on the earth as a whole and on us as individuals. The moon represents the dark, the hidden, and the mysterious. Let me clarify one thing here. Dark does not mean evil. It simply means unseen, in the shadows, the night. The sun represents the day and the light, the moon represents the night and the dark. It also represents those qualities within us, our personal shadows, voids and secrets that we keep hidden deep within ourselves. During the esbats, these are the depths that we explore.

An esbat is any ritual or celebration that is based on the lunar cycle. It doesn't matter whether you're dancing in celebration by the light of the full moon, performing a ritual for new growth at new moon, or taking an inward meditative journey during dark moon. If your activity was scheduled according to a specific lunar phase, it is an esbat.

This chapter illustrates the teachings of the Lunae tradition that my students have found to be useful when trying to understand and work with the energies of the lunar cycle.

The most basic astronomical phases of that cycle are:

Dark Moon – the moon and sun are in conjunction. The sun is behind the moon relative to the earth, causing the moon's face to remain unlit. The time of the dark moon runs from the moment after that last sliver of waning moon has disappeared until the moment before the new moon becomes visible.

New Moon – the moment the moon moves out of conjunction with the sun and the first sliver of the moon's backward "C" shaped crescent is visible anywhere on the earth.

Full Moon – the moon and sun are in opposition. This simply means that the sun and the moon are directly opposite each other relative to the earth, causing the entire face of the moon to be brightly lit.

Waning Moon – from the moment of the full moon until the moment when the last sliver of the moon's "C" shaped crescent is visible. It is called this because the visible crescent shrinks or "wanes".

Waxing Moon – from the moment of the new moon until the moment when the moon becomes full. It is called this because the visible crescent grows or "waxes".

<u>Dark Moon</u>

Astronomically speaking, the dark moon is the period of time (roughly three days) in which the sun and moon are in conjunction. If you were to draw a straight line between the earth and the sun at this time, it would pass through the moon. The moon sits between the earth and the sun, causing the hemisphere of the moon that faces us to remain dark. The sky is devoid of moonlight.

But what does the time of the Dark Moon mean? What do we use it for?

The moon represents mystery. During the dark of the moon, the sky is left with a void where the moonlight normally reigns. The moon rules our emotions. The dark represents that which is hidden. Now take all of those statements and consider them together. The Dark Moon symbolizes the hidden, mysterious voids within us. Hidden, most often, from our conscious minds because they are things that we lack emotionally and they can be quite painful to discover and face.

I'm not talking about something that you once had, but lost. The voids are that which you have never had or been capable of. Let me use myself as an example. There are social skills that I lack because I have a basic, emotional fear of people as a group. I am incapable of making small talk. It's an ability I have never possessed.

I have been a public speaker, a teacher, group leader and even a performer. I have no fear of standing in front of a large group of people because I never do it without being completely prepared on my given subject matter. However, after my presentation is finished, there always seems to be a period of "meet and greet". This causes me a great deal of emotional anxiety. My palms sweat, my knees shake and a large knot forms in my stomach. All of this occurs simply because I lack the basic ability to make small talk and chitchat with people whom I do not know. This is one of my "voids".

We all have voids, things we lack the ability to do. Have you ever wanted to play a musical instrument, paint, sky dive or parasail? Why don't you? These are what I call "ability voids". Things we don't we possess the knowledge to do or perhaps have a hidden emotional fear of doing. If you tried skydiving and didn't like it, then that would be a valid reason for not doing it again. You possess the ability and the training, but it just isn't what you want to do. A void is not having the ability to do something in order to evaluate its place in your life, physically or emotionally.

Have you ever met someone who was so emotionally distant that you felt daunted or instantly pushed away? Maybe that person has purposely created that distance due to some emotional memory or event. Consider this, however. Perhaps that person has never possessed the ability to become emotionally bonded or close with another person.

We aren't born emotionally schooled. We are taught, by those who raise us and by society in general, how to initiate and conduct interpersonal relationships. What happens if no one teaches you? Then it becomes a void, an ability you never learned and do not possess. This is what the Dark Moon symbolizes. It represents the internal and external voids in our lives; the things we don't even realize are missing because we never experienced their presence in the first place.

The time of the Dark Moon is meant for exploration deep within ourselves to discover what we don't have, what our voids are, and how to fill them. Facing our inner selves is difficult. It takes courage to seek out what the subconscious mind works so hard to hide from us. It requires you to be completely honest with yourself and, in order to do this, you must have a passionate desire to seek the truth. This is not a journey that one can make easily or take lightly.

New Moon

The new moon is the first moment the moon moves out of conjunction with the sun and the first sliver of the moon's backward "C" shaped crescent is visible from the earth.

What does this lunar phase mean and how do we use its energy?

The New Moon is all about beginnings. As the moon begins a new cycle of light, we begin new things. We plant seeds, begin new projects, work spells to draw things to us and do meditations to understand and enrich our inner, spiritual lives. These efforts continue throughout the waxing phase. As the moon's lighted face grows, so grow our seeds and works.

This is the time to start new thought processes or simply clear out the mental cobwebs. Is there an important conversation that you've been putting off, hoping for that "right time" to bring up a delicate topic? Is it time for a mental conversation with yourself about a new direction you'd like to take in your life? Do you want or need to change the focus of your thoughts and energies? New Moon is a great time for these things.

It's a good time to make physical changes in your life as well. Major purchases, such as a new house or car, tend to go smoother and be more hassle-free around the New Moon. Maybe you've wanted to take a trip, ask for a raise, or even find a new job altogether. Perhaps it's a lifestyle change you would like to make – start a new diet or exercise plan, move in with your partner or get married. These are all new beginnings and that's what the time of the New Moon is all about.

New Moon is also a wonderful time to begin new projects. If the season is right, you could literally plant some new seeds and start an herb, vegetable or flower garden. Start a new artistic endeavor. Carve a statue, write a poem, create a collage, design and sew a new shirt, maybe do some beading or drawing. Perhaps you like building things – get that hammer out, grab some nails, and build a birdhouse or a bookcase.

The time of the New Moon is meant for doing. It's the time to get up, shake off the dust, and start over fresh or begin something totally new.

Full Moon

The full moon is the moment when the moon and sun are in opposition. This simply means that the sun and the moon are directly opposite each other relative to the earth, causing the entire face of the moon to be brightly lit. If you were to draw a straight line between the sun and the moon at this time, it would pass through the earth as it lies between the two.

What does this phase mean and how can we use its energies?

At the Full Moon, we celebrate the fruition of the efforts begun at New Moon. Just as the moon is now full and bright, so, too, are we. It is the time of harvests and gratitude. We would all do well to remember to be grateful, whether or not our workings and efforts have been successful. Waking up each morning is enough reason to be grateful, in my opinion.

A large part of being truly grateful is to focus on what we have rather than what we lack. This is the time to literally count your blessings and be thankful for your personal harvests – physical, emotional, intellectual, and spiritual. Celebrate any lessons you've learned and challenges you've completed, no matter how easy or difficult they were. This is also a time to use external magic, such as healings, cleansing or consecrating of tools, or doing works for others.

Waxing Moon

The crescent of light visible on the face of the moon grows during the waxing phase, so we grow things in our lives as well. The seeds we planted at New Moon have begun to stir and sprout, so this is the period of time when we focus on tending and nurturing the new growths in our lives in order to ensure a full and productive harvest at Full Moon.

Waning Moon

During the waning phase, just as the moon appears to be shedding its light, we shed things from our lives as well. Meditations and spell works are done to remove negative, harmful or unnecessary people, behaviors and influences from our surroundings. We clean our spiritual house.

7

Tools

There is one important thing to remember when learning about the tools of Wicca and/or witchcraft.

Tools aren't necessary.

This is one of the things that many people struggle with. The power is in the practitioner. You don't need any specific tool to commune with the deities. You don't need any tool to work with the energies and beings of the various elements. You certainly don't need any tool to help you raise energy or work a spell. Tools can certainly be helpful at times, but they aren't necessary at all.

Your energy, mind, spirit, heart, intent – these are the things that are required to practice Wicca and to work magic. Sometimes the simpler you make things, the better it works. There are even times when all the tools can just get in the way.

If you choose to use them, the tools do serve a purpose. They can help you to focus more clearly or to gain better control of various energies. The following is one example that illustrates why we use tools and how they can be helpful.

Think about cooking. Three hundred years ago there were no gas or electric stoves, no microwave or convection ovens. Women had to cook food over wood fires. This was hard work. It required chopping down trees, cutting the logs into usable pieces, carrying large numbers of pieces over sometimes great distances, building the fire, etc. You get the picture. Even though they didn't have the conveniences that we do, they still got the job done fairly effectively.

Now think about how much quicker and easier cooking that same meal is for us because of the more efficient tools we have. We can do the exact same things with less work and more output. It's the same with the tools of Wicca and witchcraft. You can accomplish whatever you need to without the tools, it's just that sometimes it's easier and more convenient to have and use them. But it's still a personal choice either way.

In the Lunae tradition, we use only those tools that are necessary and only when their use feels appropriate to the ritual or working at hand. Here is a list of our tools and their purposes:

Altar – a table or other working surface that holds tools and supplies.
Altar cloth – used to cover the altar before laying out tools and may be tailored to a specific sabbat or ritual purpose.
Bowl – used to hold loose incense, salt or supplies to be used during the ritual.
Besom – a broom used to symbolically cleanse the ritual area prior to casting or bringing up the circle.

Book of Shadows – a collection of writings that is kept to chronicle the magical workings or collective journey of the coven. Ours contains information on spells, rituals, recipes, workings, and coven gatherings.

Candles – used as representations of deity and the elements, and may be lit to signify their arrivals when called. Appropriately colored candles are also used during various magical workings.

Cauldron – one is three inches wide and holds the water, representing the element of Water, to which salt will be added to create holy water. The other is ten inches wide and is used in magical workings. Both are made from cast iron and used to represent the cycles of life, death and rebirth.

Censer – used to hold the smoldering charcoal, representing the element of Fire, to which incense will be added to create holy smoke.

Chalice – a cup bearing our coven sigil which holds the liquid offering for the simple feast.

Deity Symbols – carved from wood and each sitting on a wooden pentacle base, we have a horned moon (round disk topped with an upturned crescent) for God and the triple moon (round disk flanked by outwardly pointing crescents) for Goddess.

Paten – A ritual plate bearing our coven sigil which holds the food offering for the simple feast.

Pentacle – a slice of felled cedar from my yard, representing the element of Earth, into which a five-pointed star has been inscribed, symbolizing the union of all the elements which create and maintain life.

8

Divination

Divination is not only used for seeing the future or conversing with spirits. Divining rods can be used for many things – detecting spirit energy, finding underground water, locating lost objects or determining where gas pipes are buried. Pendulums can be used much in the same way. A perfect example would be putting a pregnant woman's ring on a chain and holding it over her belly to discover the baby's gender by observing how it swings. Scrying has been used for centuries by almost every society in the world. The famous quatrains of Nostradamus were reportedly written as a result of his scrying efforts. Some methods of divination can be used to view the past and present, as well as the future.

Following is a list of some types of divination with explanations of what they are. I've given history, usage ideas, and other information for some of the more commonly used methods.

Crystallomancy, also known as crystal gazing, is the divining of events by gazing into a glass, polished rock or crystal ball. Druids are one of the earliest known peoples to have used crystals in divination, beginning as far back as 2,000 BCE. During the Medieval Period in Europe, seers, wizards, gypsies and fortune tellers also used crystals to see into the past, present or future. Due to its transparent nature, beryl was often used in the divination process. Scottish Highlanders called these "stones of power".

Later, other types of rock crystal or transparent rocks began to be used. Seer stones were even used early in the history of Mormonism. Joseph Smith, Jr. was known to have used stones and crystals to receive scriptures or revelations from God. Several Mormon texts refer to prophets using these seer stones to receive direction and revelations. Crystal gazing has been used by many cultures around the world throughout the ages.

This is one method of divination that is easily adapted to the type of answer that you are seeking. Looking for spiritual guidance? Try gazing into a large amethyst crystal or ball. Do you want to see events coming that you might need to protect yourself from? Citrine is perfect for that. Maybe you would like to take a look at a previous life or two. Why not try some clear or lilac Kunzite? Any stone or crystal that has a natural reflective surface, or can be polished to produce one, can be used to scry with.

Simply prepare yourself as you would for meditation. Comfortable clothes, appropriate music if you like, perhaps burn corresponding or enhancing incense, and find a sitting position that works for you and allows the crystal to be at or slightly below eye level. Light some candles, dim the lights and focus. Eventually you may begin to see images, words or movement within the crystal. However, don't be discouraged if you are not successful on your first attempt. Like anything else, crystal gazing takes practice and concentration. Play with it and never be afraid to experiment to find what works best for you.

Pyromancy comes from the Greek words 'pyros', meaning fire, and 'manteia', meaning divination. Thus, it literally means divining by means of fire. Since fire has been an important component of society since the earliest of times, it seems likely that pyromancy is one of the oldest forms of divination. Fire is fascinating and fluid, colorful and ever changing, and so easily holds one's gaze and attention. It has been written that the virgins at the Temple of Athena regularly practiced pyromancy, as did the followers of Hephaestus, the god of fire and forge. In ancient China, various dynasties are known to have practiced pyromancy by burning or heating oracle bones, generally the shoulder blade of an ox or sometimes a tortoise shell, to produce cracks which were then read for omens and portents. Using bones specifically is known as **osteomancy**. Inscriptions on some of these oracle bones are among the earliest known examples of Chinese writing.

The most basic form of pyromancy is, of course, the reading of shapes and signs within the flames themselves, whether from a bonfire, hearth fire or candle flame. However, there are several variations that I feel are worth mentioning. **Alomancy** is divination by means of casting salt into a fire and reading the signs or symbols left in the residue when the fire has burned out. **Botanomancy** is the burning of plants within the fire and **daphnomancy** is specifically the burning of laurel leaves for divination. Divining signs within the smoke of a fire is **capnomancy** and the use of burning straw is known specifically as **sideromancy**.

Hydromancy, also known as ydromancy and hydrascopy, is the name given to various different methods of divination by means of water or rain. There are many different techniques and methods that fall under the umbrella of hydromancy.

Lecanomancy is a form of hydromancy developed by ancient Assyrians. It consists of interpreting the patterns and ripples on the surface of water that has had precious stones dropped into it. This form of water divination is also tied to wishing wells. It was thought that if you dropped a coin into water and made a wish on it, you could read the answer to your wish in the ripples and patterns produced by the dropping of the coin.

Castronomancy is the process of divining by looking into images on the surface of water in a glass or magical receptacle, such as a scrying bowl. Some people prefer to color the water with black ink to provide a more reflective surface and to somewhat eliminate ordinary reflections. If a sacred spring or pool is used, or if spring water is placed in the scrying bowl, this is known as **pegomancy**. It is said that Nostradamus used a bowl of water, darkened with black ink, to scry for the images and visions that he recorded in his famous quatrains. Even the Wicked Witch in "The Wizard of Oz" used the liquid in her cauldron as a means of scrying, to watch the activities of her nemesis, Dorothy.

Ancient Persians developed and used another type of water scrying called **eromanty**. This involved the diviner enveloping his or her head in a napkin, filling a vase with water and then exposing that vase to the open air. The diviner would whisper questions over the vase. If the surface of the water then showed bubbles, it was taken as a positive or affirmative answer to the question.

Hydromancy is one of the oldest forms of scrying, mainly because it requires no special tools really, and anyone who is patient and open is capable of seeing signs, symbols and omens in the depths of the water. Water flows just as time does. If we are diligent, patient and perceptive enough, it may show us images of where it has been and where it yet will go.

Cleromancy consists of casting lots, whether with sticks, bones, beans or some other items. Modern playing cards and board games developed from this type of divination.

Bibliomancy is a type of divination in which a question is asked and then the Bible is opened randomly. The answer is contained within the first passage that catches the eye. Variations include using any book or text in the same manner. The I Ching is a combination of bibliomancy and cleromancy.

Astrology is the means of divining answers using celestial bodies and relationships.

Ailuromancy or **felidomancy** uses the observance of feline behavior.

Cartomancy is the use of playing cards, tarot cards or oracle cards.

Cheiromancy or **palmistry** is the art of reading the lines and features of one or both palms to divine past, present or future events.

Dactylomancy is divination by means of finger movements upon tripods, planchettes, pendulums, Ouija boards or through the use of finger rings.

Extispicy is reading the entrails of ritually sacrificed animals.

Geomancy, which includes Feng Shui divination, is the interpretation of markings on the ground or how a handful of dirt lands when tossed.

Graphology is the interpretation of handwriting.

Numerology is the system of divining by numbers or number combinations.

Oneiromancy is divination through dream interpretation.

Onomancy is the method of divining by using names, commonly used in conjunction with numerology.

Podomancy is similar to palmistry, but reads instead the lines and features of the soles of one or both feet.

Phrenology is the study of the shape of a person's skull.

Scatomancy is the art of studying animal droppings for signs and omens.

Taromancy is the specific form of cartomancy in which one uses tarot cards.

9

Circle Casting and Invitations

Let's start with an important question – why cast circle at all? Here are some typical examples of reasons to cast a circle:

- To create a separate sacred space
- To delineate the working area
- To contain or concentrate raised energy
- To separate magical and mundane selves

The act of creating a circle requires concentration and focus because you are manipulating and forming energy. The steps needed to do this can help us to clear our minds of everyday concerns, allowing us to achieve greater focus and concentration in our magical workings. I call this the separation of magical and mundane selves.

Some people cast circle only when they're going to perform ritual, some never cast circle at all. If you have the ability to just drop all your worldly cares at a moment's notice, then more power to you. Most can't do it that simply and need additional help to focus.

Many believe that you must cast a magical circle prior to any ritual in order to protect yourself and your workings from outside interference. I do not agree and I will quote my grandmother's thoughts on this as my reasoning behind this opinion. She told me, "If you ain't a good enough witch, if you ain't big enough to keep control, then you probably shouldn't ought to be working magic, now should you?"

Ok, I've decided that I want to cast circle – what now? How exactly do I do that? First of all, it's important to realize that you're not creating just a circle, in reality you need to create a sphere. If you simply create a one-dimensional circle on the ground, then it affects only the flat area contained within that flat circle. Basically what's involved is this – you use energy to create a sphere around the space you want to enclose. An easy example of how to accomplish this is to draw a circle of energy on the ground, then expand it above and below you to form a sphere.

To get an idea of what this energy sphere should resemble, visualize a coconut. Now imagine that coconut cut in half – this represents the top and bottom halves of your sphere, an energy 'shell'. If you put the two pieces back together, but this time with a piece of paper between them, the paper would represent the surface you're standing on. This places just as much space above that line as there is below it, which is what you want in your sphere.

There is an exception to this however. If you live in a second floor apartment or are creating your circle in an upstairs room, you may not want your sphere to extend below you like that, especially if it might impose on someone else's personal space. In a case like that, it's perfectly acceptable to only create the upper portion of the sphere to keep it contained to your own space, but remember to include the floor that you're standing on as well.

You can use any tool you find appropriate to direct the energy to create the circle, such as an athame, wand or your finger. You may choose not to use any other tool than your mind and simply visualize the creation. Casting circle is a very personal process and you may have to try a few different methods until you find what feels right and best suits you.

When calling the four elements, it's generally best to decide first what you want to invite and what you want it to do or add to your ritual. What you call in will often depend on what you need. It is generally better to begin with something small, an easily visualized and managed representation of the element, and then move on to more advanced energies as your abilities grow.

Simple element energy is the most basic form, without the capacity for higher thought and reasoning, such as stones, plants, insects or colors. This could also include physical manifestations of the elements such as wind, rain or mountains.

Elementals are beings that are capable of reasoning or have a will of their own. These would include animals, ancestors, fairies, mermaids, gnomes, or even specific deities. When calling in an elemental, you should be prepared to issue specific instructions regarding what you are asking of it.

Here is an example of how to apply this information. Let's say that I'm going to do a Full Moon ritual, during which I'm going to work a healing spell for a friend with pneumonia (I have permission, of course). I only want to call in small things, but I want them to add their energies to the spell to make it stronger.

Here are the quarter calls I might use:

East – (visualize streamers blowing in the wind) Air, I ask you to join me and bring gentle breezes to refresh both mind and lungs.

South – (visualize a campfire) Fire, I ask you to join me and help to ease the fever and strengthen the will.

West – (visualize a small stream) Water, I ask you to join me and to bring the purifying flow to wash away all infection.

North – (visualize a strong tree) Earth, I ask you to join me and help to stabilize and strengthen the body.

Things to remember when calling the quarters:

Presence or witness only – may either stand outside or be invited into the circle

Limited participation or celebration – invited within the circle and must be given specific directions

Active participant – invited within the circle, asked to bring specific energies with it, expected to fully participate in the ritual activities

Always remember to convey your thanks and appreciation prior to issuing farewells. A hurt or irritated elemental can be mischievous and/or rude. Also, don't invite anything that is beyond your ability to control. If you bring it in, you must be capable of sending it away.

Once you've finished your entire ritual – now what? Now it's time to dismantle your circle. There are many things you can do at this point, depending on your circumstances. If you used an athame or wand to direct the energy during creation, you can simply pull the energy back into the tool and store it there until the next time you want to create circle. Using this method tends to build up and stabilize the energy a little more each time.

If you have a permanent ritual area in your home, you could choose to leave the energy in place by simply opening a seam at the top of the sphere and collapsing the sides down into the ground. The bottom half of the sphere can stay in place at all times. This is the method that we use at JKL. To cast circle the next time, we simply pull up some of the existing energy and reform the top half of the sphere. You could also choose to walk around the circle, dispersing the energy back out into the universe as you go or pushing it out to the edges of your property line to strengthen and reinforce any magical boundaries you may have in place.

10

Raising Energy

Why and how do we raise energy? Once we figure that out, how can we direct and use it? What should be done with any leftovers when you're finished?

Why would we want to raise energy in the first place? It isn't necessary to raise specific energy at all, but there are definitely times that it can be quite useful and serve a specific purpose for us.

Some of the reasons to raise energy are:

- To empower any spell work being done
- To heal ourselves or to help others to heal
- To send to others in times of need or crisis
- In celebration of a specific date or event

Where can we get that energy from? The energy of the universe is everywhere, surrounding us at all times, just waiting to be drawn from and used. Some possible sources to consider and methods for tapping into it are:

Pull it up from the earth – visualize roots growing down from your feet to channel up the natural earth energy.

Pull it in from the circle itself – we often pull balls or streamers of energy from the sphere that we've already created.

Pull it down from the moon or sun – we have a joyous Full Moon ritual that we perform on a regular basis where we visualize streamers of light flowing down from the moon and into our heart centers. We then leap and dance around the circle, weaving these streamers into a beautiful tapestry of celebration.

Draw it in from the space around you – swirl the energy of the air into balls or streamers that can be directed to where you need them.

Draw it in from the universe – similar to the method that Reiki practitioners use, allowing the energy of the universe to flow through the body like a pipeline and simply direct, via the hand chakras, where that energy flows to.

An important part of raising energy is determining what method will help you to maintain your focus. It's also good to have an idea of how much energy will be sufficient for what you're doing. Once you've determined those things, how do you then build up and direct that energy where you want it go?

Some useful methods for raising and focusing that energy are:

- Dancing
- Singing or chanting
- Drumming
- Meditation
- Channel through one or more of your chakras
- Pull it into and channel it through a wand or athame
- Control and focus it with your hands
- Control and focus it with your mind through visualization

You've raised the energy, completed any workings, and the ritual is almost finished. What now? What can you do with any remaining or excess energy?

You could ground the excess, using the roots visualization, but this time reversing the flow and giving the excess back to the earth. You could always store it in a statue, wand or athame to use at a later time. Another good idea is to simply use it to refresh and energize your body. Or you could send it out – push it up and out of the circle with the intention that it should go where it's needed most.

There is one caution that I always issue to anyone intending to raise energy for any purpose.

Never use your own energy when you can raise it from another source!!

I can't emphasize that strongly enough. It would serve no useful purpose to deplete yourself when you don't need to. What good does it do to work a healing spell for someone else if it only makes you ill as a result? Then you would have to do yet another working to raise energy from an outside source in order to heal yourself. There's no need for you to suffer when you can avoid the problem by simply going straight to the outside source from the beginning.

This doesn't mean that the process is impersonal either. You're still putting in your intentions. You're still the one shaping that energy, directing its use and forming the intentional outcome that it will provide. You simply won't be draining your own resources during the process.

11

Spell Work

What exactly is spell work? The word "spell" comes from the Middle English "spleen" and the Old English "spelian", both of which mean to represent or substitute for. Objects such as stones, herbs, and candles are used to represent the various elemental attributes that we want to incorporate into any magical working. Similarly, the charms that you write or speak (the specific words you use) represent the personal intentions that you are adding to the working. Therefore, spell work is the use of objects or words specifically geared toward obtaining a particular goal.

Many world religions have practices that accomplish the same thing, but under a different name. When a Christian goes to their church, lights a candle and says a prayer to ask that someone be healed of an illness, it's essentially no different than what a Wiccan would do in the same situation. I might choose a specific color of candle that I feel would be most helpful or write my words down beforehand rather than make it up as I go along, but it all amounts to the same thing. It's a process of focusing our needs and intentions in order to send a clear message to deity of what we desire and then ask for their help in accomplishing it. A prayer and a spell are one and the same, directed to the same destination. It's only the specific trappings of that prayer which change from religion to religion and from practitioner to practitioner.

A question I'm often asked is whether or not there are specific rules or requirements that must be followed in order for a spell to be successful. Must there be a written or spoken charm for it to be effective? Is there a magical formula for writing a charm that will make it foolproof?

The simple answer is no.

Are there steps you can take or things you can do in order to focus your intentions more clearly? Definitely! The more clearly defined your goals and intentions, the more focused your energy, the more successful you'll be.

Here are some of the simple steps you could take to help improve the flow and focus of any working:

Gather everything that you'll need beforehand and place it all somewhere close and convenient to your working surface. Your spell work may not be as effective if you have to go looking for something you need after you're already in the middle of the working.

Have any charm or chant that you want to use written down. It can seriously disrupt your focus and the working flow if you have to stop in the middle of everything and figure out exactly what you want to say.

A time-saving tip is to cleanse, bless and/or consecrate all of the spell components at once, prior to beginning the actual working. Not only does it save time, but it also ensures that you don't forget or leave out any individual component.

Another question I've encountered is whether or not to do some type of divination prior to spell work in order to determine if a favorable outcome is expected or if the working should be done at another time. My answer is always the same. If you doubt the outcome of the working before you've even started, why bother to do it at all? Trust in your own abilities and in the validity of the working is absolutely the most important and valuable ingredient to have! This leads straight to a key point I'd like make.

You need nothing more than your heart and mind to work a spell.

You don't have to light a candle to have a prayer heard and you certainly don't have to sew a poppet or go through an elaborate ritual to accomplish a magical working. Yes, these can definitely be useful, but no tools are ever absolutely necessary. A sincere desire, an honest intention, and your words (written, spoken or thought) are all you need to be truly successful in your magical spell work.

12

Ritual

This chapter is about the ritual as a whole – the steps for planning, preparing and carrying out any ritual. What are rituals, what do they do for us, and what do we need to think about and consider before we do an actual ritual?

The word "ritual" means:

1. The established form for a ceremony
2. An act or series of acts regularly repeated in a set precise manner

Examples of mundane rituals that everyone does every day:

1. Morning preparations
2. Night time preparations
3. Routine job actions

Some of the reasons we perform ritual activities, both magical and mundane:

1. Focus
2. Formality
3. Tradition
4. Familiarity
5. Memory

Some purposes that rituals serve:

1. Comfort
2. Mindset
3. Focus

The first step in planning a ritual is to decide what the intent or purpose of your ritual will be – celebrating a sabbat or full moon, a general "thank you", or an energy working of some kind.

The next step is deciding on the level of formality. Do you want to just create sacred space to dance under the moon or do you want to add in all the bells and whistles to do a dramatic, full-blown ritual?

Next you need to consider what actions you're going to take during the ritual, such as performing spell work, energy raising, drumming, dancing, etc.

Decide what to you're going to call in - what are you calling for corners, are you calling specific deities?

When and where are you doing this? Are you going to hold your ritual during waning or waxing moon phase, on a particular day of the week, on a sabbat? Do you want to hold it outside or will your living room be fine?

An important step is then to gather together all the tools you want to use during the ritual. If you're doing spell work, then it's important to have your herbs, candles, stones and other necessary items together and where you'll want them once you cast your circle or create sacred space. Nothing is more frustrating than having to ruin your concentration and go searching for something you need in the middle of a ritual.

Purification process and ritual wear – should you take a purification bath prior to beginning your ritual, do you want to use ritual clothes or special jewelry, etc.

How you intend to release the elements and deities you called in and determining whether or not they've actually gone.

What to do if they haven't left yet.

What to do with the energy of the circle – dismantle it, push it to the edges of the property, store it in a statue until next time, store in your athame, etc.

You've planned everything out now, so how do you get started? What's described here is the format of a Lunae ritual, the progression of events and why we include each step. Ritual is a tool that we use to focus our minds on the task at hand and accomplish a specific goal. The steps of a ritual are designed to create a natural progression of events that help us to leave behind the laundry, the stress of our jobs, the burned dinner, and all the other million and one distractions that occupy our thoughts constantly and interfere with our concentration. And, like any exercise that raises and expends energy, ritual is designed to have a warm-up, energetic phase, and a cool-down period.

The parts of a ritual are:

- Purification bath
- Circle creation
- Consecration and devotion of the elements
- Circle consecration
- Calling in the elements
- Inviting or invoking deity
- Enacting purpose
- Raising energy
- Simple Feast
- Deity farewells
- Element farewells
- Circle release

Let's look at each of these steps individually.

Purification Bath

The purification bath is an important first step in any ritual process. If you think about it, the bathtub is a very spiritual place. Add salt, oils, herbs or flowers to the bathwater and it is a place where all the elements can combine to cleanse, purify and ground us on a physical and spiritual level. Fire heats the Water. Water washes away the physical and spiritual 'dust' that clings to us. Water combines with Air, Earth (herbs, salt and flowers) and Fire (oils) to create steam filled with the scents and attributes of the added ingredients – opening our pores and sinuses, as well as stimulating the mind and senses. We can cleanse and consecrate ritual space and tools more effectively if we have cleansed and consecrated ourselves first.

Circle Creation

We can create our circle using one of the methods discussed in chapter 9.

Consecration and Devotion of the Elements

This is where we cleanse, consecrate and devote the salt, water, incense and censer (with lighted charcoal) for sacred or ritual use. To consecrate simply means 'to make holy'. The following is an example of how this might be accomplished in the Lunae tradition.

Take the chalice or bowl of water and first touch it to the altar pentacle to ground it. It is then held in one hand, placing the other hand over the top of it and visualizing cleansing white light streaming into the water to purify it. At the same time, acknowledging a connection to that element by saying, "I am of the Water, through which I am reborn", devotes the now cleansed water for spiritual use. Set the water down on the pentacle, pick up the bowl of salt, touch it to the pentacle as well, cleansing and devoting it via the same process while saying "I am of the Earth which is my strength." Take a pinch of the salt and sprinkle it into the water in a deosil (clock-wise) direction three times, then stir in a deosil direction three times with an index finger. Hold the bowl of water up toward the moon and consecrate it for sacred use, asking Goddess to make it holy by saying, "Great Mother, I give you honor." Set the holy water aside and move to the next element. Pick up the censer (containing previously lighted charcoal), touching it to the pentacle, cleansing and devoting it in the same manner as before, while saying "I am of the Fire which is my passion." Set it on the pentacle, pick up the bowl (or cone) of incense, touch it to the pentacle, cleansing and devoting it while saying "I am of the Air which is my breath." Place the incense into the censer. Hold the censer up toward the sun and consecrate it for sacred use, asking God to make it holy by saying, "Great Father, I give you honor."

Circle Consecration

In the Rede, it directs us to "walk the circle thrice about". You've already walked it (either literally or figuratively) once when you created it. As a representative of deity incarnate, we view this as adding the energy of Spirit to the circle.

Now you will walk it for the second time. Take your chalice or bowl of holy water and walk the circle in a deosil path, sprinkling as you go. You are adding the consecrated energies and attributes of Water and Earth to the energy of the circle already in place, strengthening it.

Then you will finish by walking the circle for the third time, carrying the censer. This will add the consecrated energies of Air and Fire in the same manner. You now have a strong, consecrated circle in which to work.

Calling in the Elements

This is the point where you call whatever representations of the elements that you chose prior to beginning, based on what you want them to do. This was discussed in chapter 9.

Inviting Deity

How you do this, what to say or do, depends largely on your own personal style, beliefs and comfort level as well as the purpose of your ritual. In the Lunae tradition, God and Goddess are invoked in the same manner used for the elements, by simply inviting them in and stating why.

An example of an invocation would be:

"Great Mother, we ask you to join us on this Full Moon night as we dance under your moon and celebrate your presence and energy in our lives."

You might choose to invite both God and Goddess in one invocation or invite them individually. Likewise, you could choose which to invite first. It's common to invite Goddess first during an Esbat (lunar) ritual and invite God first in a Sabbat (solar) ritual because of the energies being celebrated.

Enacting Purpose

Now it's time for the work, the fun and the meat of the ritual! This is where you will perform your magical workings, spell work, healing work, give your speech of thanks or whatever else the purpose of your ritual may be.

Raising Energy

Many choose to skip this particular step, preferring to pour energy into their spells and charms as they create them. Some, however, choose to put together a charm bag, amulet or talisman first, and then raise the power to charge it. This was discussed in chapter 10.

Simple Feast

You may have also seen this referred to as "Cakes and Ale". The cakes can be anything made from any grain product, and the ale can be anything wet.

Simple feast serves two purposes – the physical act of eating helps to ground us after working magic, beginning our return to everyday concerns, and it also serves as a time to give thanks for the physical sustenance provided for us. It should always be remembered to reserve a portion of the food and drink to be returned to the earth after the ritual. This is done as a symbolic giving back or sharing, a gesture to indicate that we promise to continue to feed the earth that feeds us. You can use any words of thanks that feel comfortable.

Deity and Element Farewells

This is where you acknowledge God and Goddess and their presence during your ritual, saying any thanks or goodbyes that you feel are appropriate. It's generally best to do it in the same manner as the invitation – if God and Goddess were invited individually, they should be thanked individually, or if both were invited together, they should be thanked together.

The elements are thanked for their presence and any assistance they've given. In the Lunae tradition, we generally say something simple to each element, such as "Go with our thanks." Refer to chapter 4 for more information on this step.

There is one thing that we practice and teach that I would like to stress here. When our invitations are issued one at a time, whether silent or aloud, they are done so in a deosil manner. The subsequent farewells are then issued in a widdershins manner. The first one in will be the last one out.
Example:

The invitations are issued in the order of Air, Fire, Water, Earth, God, and Goddess.

The farewells are then issued in the order of Goddess, God, Earth, Water, Fire, and Air.

Circle Release

There are as many ways to take down a circle as there are to create one. This is discussed in chapter 9.

The following is the officially accepted and sanctioned method by which a Lunae ritual is conducted.

Ritual Steps

1. Altar Tool Placements
    a. Tools are used at the discretion of the ritual leader.
    b. Always placed on left (if used):
        i. God symbol
        ii. God candle
        iii. Lighter
        iv. Censer
        v. Incense (there is a specific coven blend to be used)
        vi. Paten (paten is non-receptive = God, holds cakes = Goddess)
        vii. Athame (ritual leader will use their own – there is no coven athame)
        viii. Blessing oil (there is a specific coven blend to be used)
    c. Always on right (if used):
        i. Goddess symbol
        ii. Goddess candle
        iii. Snuffer

        iv.   Cauldron of water

        v.   Bowl of salt

        vi.   Wand

        vii.   Chalice (chalice is receptive = Goddess, holds ale = God)

   d.   Pentacle is centered in the front – closest to the ritual leader.

   e.   Use of corner symbols is at the discretion of the ritual leader. Stones, candles or other corner symbols may be used. If using candles, lighters in the corresponding colors and snuffers should be placed at the corners as well.

   f.   CD player and music may be used at the discretion of the ritual leader.

2. Circle Creation

   a.   The purpose of circle creation is to:

        i.   Create a space separate and apart that is designated for religious use only.

        ii.   Combine or unite the energies of those present.

        iii.   Create a boundary to contain any energy raised.

   b.   Must use the coven circle if available. This may be done on any part of the Covenstead property by raising the existing coven energy from the ground to complete the sphere around the participants.

   c.   If not available (such as holding ritual off Covenstead property), circle must be created with energy prior to moving on to step 3.

    d. Even if using the coven circle, the ritual leader may also choose to create an additional or separate circle of energy.

3. Cleansings, Devotions, Consecrations

    a. The use of cleansings, devotions and consecrations is not necessary unless creating a new circle, but must be done any time that elemental representations, such as the censer and incense, are used on the altar.

    b. There are no official coven devotions and/or consecrations – may be performed by the ritual leader according to their preference.

    c. Cleansings, devotions and consecrations may be performed silently or aloud.

    d. Required order is:

        i. Cleanse and devote water

        ii. Cleanse and devote salt

        iii. Add salt to water, stirring 3 times in a deosil direction

        iv. Goddess devotion then consecrates

        v. Cleanse and devote censer

        vi. Cleanse and devote incense

        vii. Add incense to censer

        viii. God devotion then consecrates

    e. Consecration of the circle must be performed following cleansing, devotion and consecration of the elements.

4. Circle Consecration
    a. The purpose of circle consecration is to use the consecrated and devoted energies of the elements to strengthen and sanctify the existing circle of energy.
    b. Consecrate circle with the energies of Water and Earth by sprinkling with holy water.
    c. Consecrate circle with the energies of Air and Fire by censing with holy smoke.
    d. Chants may accompany the consecrations at the discretion of the ritual leader.
5. Calls and Invitations
    a. The purpose of corner calls and deity invitations is to have the Elements, God and Goddess join the coven in circle to:
        i. Celebrate with us.
        ii. Witness our rites and activities.
        iii. Add their energies to our workings.
    b. Corners are called first, followed by invitations to deity.
    c. Calls and invitations may be performed silently or aloud.
    d. Must proceed in a deosil direction.
    e. Starting corner is at the discretion of the ritual leader.
    f. Do not move on to the next corner until sure that the current element has arrived.

g. The order in which deity is invited is at the discretion of the ritual leader, generally based upon the purpose of the ritual.

h. The coven has no patron deities. Choice of deities invited is at the discretion of the ritual leader.

Workings

i. This may include, but is not limited to:
   i. Sabbat celebrations
   ii. Spell work of any kind
   iii. Meditation
   iv. Healing work
   v. Energy work
   vi. Educational activities

6. Releases

   a. The purpose of releases is to avoid the accidents and incidents that can result from elemental energies running around undirected on the property after having been built up or excited during the ritual.

   b. Should be done in a widdershins direction, beginning with the last deity invited and ending with the first corner called.

   c. Each of the energies must be thanked before it is released.

   d. Do not move on to the next corner until sure the current one has gone.

e. Circle must be released in some manner.

    i. If using the coven circle, it will be placed back into the ground from which it was raised.

    ii. If a new or additional circle has been created on the Covenstead, its energy may be added to the coven circle by placing it into the ground or disbursed in some manner.

    iii. If not on Covenstead property, the circle must be taken up or dismantled by walking around it in a widdershins direction and releasing it into the universe.

7. Simple Feast

    a. The purposes of simple feast are:

        i. Grounding excess energy from the working.

        ii. To thank deity for the blessings of sustenance and to share those blessings with each other.

    b. Must include both cakes and ale.

    c. "Cakes" is defined as a food made from some kind of grain product. The food may consist of items such as:

        i. Crackers

        ii. Cookies

        iii. Snack cakes

        iv. Brownies

     v.   Any type of bread

     vi.   Special items may be allowed if deemed appropriate by the coven, but must be approved of prior to the ritual.

d.   "Ale" is not required to be alcoholic, but alcohol is allowed. The libation may consist of drinks such as:

     i.   Ale

     ii.   Beer

     iii.   Mead

     iv.   Wine

     v.   Fruit juices

     vi.   Drinks such as lemonade, tea or fruit punch

e.   Cakes and ale may be blessed and dedicated at an earlier point during ritual, but will be consumed after the releases are completed, with a portion of each reserved for step 9.

8. Returning

a.   All elemental representations from the altar will be returned to the earth. At the Covenstead, this is accomplished by scattering them under the designated tree.

b.   The reserved portion of the simple feast will be distributed in the same manner. This is done not only to return their energies to the earth, but also as a way of physically sharing the simple feast with God, Goddess and the creatures of the earth.

9. Clean up
    a. All containers will be washed or rinsed. This includes:
        i. Water cauldron
        ii. Salt bowl
        iii. Paten
        iv. Chalice
    b. The censer will be placed in a safe area until the charcoal has burned out. At the Covenstead, the censer will be placed on the stove in the kitchen. All tools will be replaced on the appropriate shelf or in the coven cabinet for storage.

13

Ethics

Most people are most familiar with at least one line from the Wiccan Rede – "An' it harm none, do as ye will". There is much more to the Rede than just that line. The first thing to know is that the word "rede" simply means "advice". The Wiccan Rede (as written by Doreen Valiente) gives common sense information intended for use as a guide – honor your ancestors and all those that came before, don't waste your time on fools, listen more than you talk, be gentle and kind with others, respect all of nature. It talks of the esbats, the sabbats, and the elements. It lists the nine sacred woods that are traditionally burned in the Beltane fire and why each is important. It tells which wood should never be burned in a magical fire. It tells how to cast the circle and make your spells more effective. It is where the Law of Return (Three-fold Law) is spelled out for us. The one line that is most commonly known is actually the very last line of the Rede, but is not its greatest part or lesson.

Wicca is a religion of respect and responsibility. We are personally responsible for our own actions, for the energy and intentions that we put out into the universe. We reap the harvest that we have planted, whether positive or negative. This is no different on a spiritual level than it is on the physical one.

Let's say that you want to plant corn, but your seeds come from plants that were blighted or diseased. You can plant as many seeds in as many rows as you like, but you'll never grow a strong and healthy crop because you started out with bad seed. With seed corn from a healthy line, you can plant fewer seeds in smaller rows and reap a bigger, healthier harvest in the end. It works the same on a magical or spiritual level. Put out strong energy with good intentions and you can harvest a bountiful crop for yourself. Put out negative energy with bad intentions – blighted and diseased results are all you're going to get out of it.

This is also a religion based on respect – for one's self, for other people, for the gods and goddesses, for Earth as a whole, and for all the creatures and energies that we share this world with. In the chapter on deity, we talked about everything coming from and being a part of the Universal One. This is why one of the foundations of Lunae Wicca is the respect for all things – we all come from and are part of the same source. We are all connected on a base energy level. If I am to pay honest respect to God and Goddess, then I must also respect all things that are a part of them or I would be lying when I say I respect the deities themselves.

Here's an example for this concept. Imagine the universe as a human body. God and Goddess are the brain; they are what keep everything else functioning smoothly together. We are the hands and feet, the part of the body that does the work needed. The plants and animals are the heart, lungs and other organs that are essential to keeping the body healthy. If we don't take care of the organs we then starve, suffocate, become toxic, etc. It doesn't matter what signals the brain sends out – if the hands and feet don't follow through, then the body dies. Now think of each hand and each foot as a separate entity (different races or religions). If the right hand decides it doesn't like the left foot – and cuts it off – guess what happens. The body bleeds to death and dies.

The Lunae tradition teaches that respect and consideration for all life is what keeps us alive and healthy on all levels – physical, spiritual and magical.

A large part of Lunae ethics concerns acting with permission, which is also a matter of respect. If we work magic on someone without their permission and knowledge, we are not respecting their right of free will and control. Even if we're trying to be helpful, we generally don't have the right to do so without asking or being asked. Life is a classroom and we are all here to learn specific lessons each time around. What if I decided before coming to this life that I needed to learn the lessons of self-respect?

Maybe I decided that to do this I would need to experience what not taking care of my body would do. Ok, I'm here and I'm dealing with some illness and learning great lessons from it – then someone comes along, works a healing spell and I'm suddenly cured. They thought they were helping me, saving me from suffering or pain. Guess what they were really doing – stopping my accomplishment and growth. Now I may have to come back in the next life and go through it all again. I'm left feeling that if I'd needed or wanted their help, I would have asked for it.

There are always exceptions to every rule, of course. One exception to the rule of permission applies to children. Most children don't have the magical or mundane means to protect or care for themselves, nor do they have the understanding and ability to give informed permission. As adults, it is one of our responsibilities to take on these tasks and to teach them to someday take on those responsibilities for themselves. It's always considered appropriate to work a healing or protection spell for a child.

Another part to consider is psychic self-defense and negative magic. By negative magic, I don't mean hexes and curses. I mean magical workings that have a negative outcome, sometimes by intention, often by accident. In other words – what happens when there is absolutely no way to "harm none", or what happens when we screw up?

There are times in the life of a practitioner when it is literally impossible to avoid causing harm of some kind. The simplest example – we all need to eat. Some vegans and vegetarians will explain that they don't eat meat or animal products (such as eggs and milk) because they can't condone any behavior which harms an animal. Well, they should really take a look at all the plant studies that have proven that plants can feel and acknowledge pain. Yes, you read that right. It has been scientifically proven that there are species of plants that react to painful stimuli by emitting high frequency sound waves – essentially they scream when cut. It's also been proven that they respond favorably to soothing touch and sound. So, no matter what we eat, we cause harm to something living in order to fuel our bodies. That, however, is the natural order of the universe. All living things participate in the unending cycle of life, death and rebirth. There's a very old saying that goes something like this – we die to feed the worms which make the soil rich to feed the plants which feed the animals which feed us who die to feed the worms…etc. It was designed to be a self-perpetuating system where all things are born, live their lives with purpose, and die with purpose as well – whether that purpose is to ensure that a member of some other species may live or simply to make room for the next generation of its own species. No matter what your choices in this life, you can't avoid causing some harm along the way.

The key is to minimize the harm you do and act from the best of intentions.

There is also the subject of self-defense. Sometimes you have to cause harm to someone else in order to protect yourself. Let's say that you're being attacked by a vicious animal. Do nothing and you're allowing harm to yourself. Hit the animal over the head with a large rock and you're causing harm to another creature. In a situation like that, it's not possible to cause absolutely no harm. Self comes first. Do as little damage as you can – if you knock the animal out on the first blow, run away. If it's unconscious and you continued to beat it with the rock until it dies, then you would be acting out of negative intentions by doing more harm than was necessary for self-preservation.

An example of how this would apply magically:

There's a rapist roaming your neighborhood, committing horrible crimes. You work a spell for him to be stopped – wait now, that's interfering with his free will. But his actions are interfering with the free will of others and causing harm. You have to decide what you can do that will cause the least harm and the most good for everyone involved.

Bad intention – do a spell to cause him to drop dead immediately.

Good intention – do a spell to bring closure and justice for the victims.

Work magic with the bad intention in mind and you're the one who'll suffer from the magical repercussions. You've done far more than was needed. Do your working with a good intention and you will get the best outcome with minimal repercussion. The result could be that he's arrested and sent to jail for the rest of his life. Yes, you've helped to interfere in his free will and done a working on him without his permission. But you've done only what was needed, with the intention of defending and protecting yourself and others.

The final negative to discuss is accidental outcomes. What happens if you make a mistake and your spell has an outcome you didn't predict and it causes harm in some way? Suck it up, learn from it, and be more specific and prepared next time. It happens to everyone at some time or another, especially in the beginning of any magical journey. We get lazy, become complacent, or don't consider all the possible outcomes, etc. Mistakes can't be avoided in magic any more than in any other part of life. Just remember that intention is everything when it comes to magic. If you didn't intend to cause something negative, the results will most likely be a cosmic slap on the hand rather than a kick in the head. Try to remember the lesson it teaches and don't make that particular mistake again if you can help it.

14

Pagan Citizenship

For us, citizenship means being a participating member of a community with all the associated rights, responsibilities and privileges. A community can be defined as a unified body of individuals, who share common interests, geographical location, cultural or historical heritage. When we look closely, we are all citizens of many communities such as our neighborhood, city, state, country, political group, etc. As Wiccans, we are citizens of the pagan and global communities as well.

Most people are well aware of the rights and privileges associated with citizenship, but few stop to think about the inherent responsibilities. As a member of our city, state and national communities, we have the right to have our voices heard. However, in order to be heard, we must exercise our responsibility to speak up. If you don't vote during an election, your voice isn't heard and choices are made for you that you may not agree with.

So what does it mean to be a good pagan citizen? It means being an active participant in this world, standing up and making your voice heard in every community in which you are a member. Get out there and vote in elections, campaign and work for projects that affect and engage you, speak out for your rights and the rights of others. Take care of your little piece of this planet.

As global citizens, we have an obligation to reduce, reuse, and recycle. As Wiccans, we hold ourselves accountable for our own actions. Part of the obligation inherent in this accountability is to contribute as little as possible to the destruction of our planet and to contribute as much as possible toward its betterment. Do what you can to reduce your carbon footprint – utilize renewable energy resources and green technologies; recycle every item you can in order to reduce what must be sent to landfills; dispose of hazardous materials such as engine oil, chemicals, paint and batteries in an appropriate matter. There are numerous resources available in print and on the internet that offer advice on sustainable living. Make use of them however and whenever you can. Take your responsibilities to yourself, your community and your planet seriously.

Community service plays a very large part in who we are and what we do. Good citizens give back to the community or group of communities that sustain them. Every year at Mabon, we hold our annual coven elections. However, who will be doing what job this year is only a small piece of what we decide that day.

Each September we choose a minimum of five community service projects that we will support or actively participate in for the coming year. There are those that we choose to support year after year, such as raising money and walking in the March of Dimes' local event, March for Babies. We do this out of gratitude that one of our coven children, who was born prematurely, is a healthy and happy little boy today.

Over the years that we have been together, we have chosen to support various food pantries, school fund drives, and other worthy charities, both in and outside of the pagan community. We ultimately started our own charitable organization in order to better serve the needs of our communities. Whether this means helping individuals and families, supporting other local charities, or facilitating events such as the local Pagan Pride Day celebration, we try to give back as much as we can as often as we can. It's who we are and what we believe, collectively, to be the right thing to do.

15

Working with Others

Once you've have learned enough about Wicca to decide whether or not you're interested in studying further and going deeper, it's time to make some important decisions. Here are some key questions which you should ask yourself at this time:

Is this a religion that I would be comfortable practicing? If you're finding conflicts between what Wicca teaches and your own core spiritual beliefs, then it isn't a good path for you. The same is true if you feel as though you would have to hide your religion from those closest to you. In order to fully blend the magical and mundane sides of your life, Wicca must be a part of who you are, not just something that you do.

Can I live within the ethical guidelines that form the basis of Wiccan principle? It can be quite an overwhelming commitment to recycle as much as possible, do your best to live in harmony with nature, reduce your carbon footprint, strive to develop stable working relationships with deity and the elements, treat people with the dignity and respect deserved as deity incarnate, be accountable for both your magical and mundane actions, and all the other myriad responsibilities that come with practicing Wicca.

If you can honestly answer yes to those two questions, then there is another set of decisions to be made.

1. Do I want to practice as a solitary, working and studying on my own?
2. Do I want to practice on my own, but find a teacher to guide my continued learning?
3. Do I want to grow and study with others in an informal setting?
4. Do I want to work and study with others in a structured setting, such as a coven?

If you choose to practice as a solitary, then you now have the basic tools to do that. There are many books and resources which you can use to continue your studies on your own.

If you would rather study with other Wiccans, but in an informal setting, you might consider forming or joining a study group. Your group could meet on a regular basis to share recipes or spells. You could designate a specific book that you'd like to study together, with each person reading the book on their own, followed by the group getting together to discuss insights and information you've individually and collectively gained. You could decide, as a group, to take your studies in any direction you wish. The key is that you would only study together. Each member of the group would continue to practice their religion individually.

There is also the option of practicing on your own and finding a teacher that would be willing to direct and guide your continued religious education, suggesting reading material or meditations that you might find helpful, answering questions on more complicated topics as you continue to learn and grow in your practice. If you choose this route as the most appropriate option for you, then there are some things to consider when choosing a teacher.

Your chosen guide should be a High Priest or High Priestess because they are generally the members of Wiccan clergy that have studied the longest, have completed the appropriate degree levels and have earned the right to teach on their own.

The High Priest or High Priestess that you consider working with should have verifiable references and be willing to provide them. You should be able to ask for and receive the name and contact information for their teacher. This is to ensure that you can not only verify their identity, but also that they have truly attained the level of High Priest or High Priestess and are qualified or authorized by their tradition to teach.

Ask to be put in contact with a few of their previous students or offer to allow your contact information to be provided to those who might want their privacy protected or anonymity maintained. You can learn a great deal about someone's ethics and teaching ability by talking with others who have studied under them.

Sit down and chat with them in person for a period of time. I would advise that this meeting last at least an hour or two. Feel out their energy. Assess their comfort level while talking to you – do they seem nervous or uncomfortable? Are you at ease in their presence?

If you ultimately decide that you'd like to work in the more structured setting of a coven, the beginning process of evaluating the High Priest or High Priestess is similar, although there are some additional questions you should consider asking at this time.

What is the coven's focus – spirituality, teaching, magic, or community service? You want to look for a group whose goals and working methods are a close fit for your own. No group is ever going to be a perfect match or provide everything you want, but the group's focus and direction should match as closely as possible if you want to build long-term magical relationships with these people.

Does the group focus on either God or Goddess, or are they considered equal? If your personal beliefs center on the concept of balance, then a predominantly God- or Goddess-oriented group probably wouldn't be the right place for you.

Do they have a degree system? Learn whether or not there is a hierarchy in place that you should be aware of. If they do have a degree system, find out how many levels it contains and if is there a testing method for attaining the various titles and advancing to the next level of training.

Once they have "passed" your initial evaluation, there are additional steps that you should take and further evaluations to be made before making a final decision and applying for membership in any coven.

Ask if it would be possible for you to attend a coven ritual. Most covens that are open to students and new members will have no problem with this and will invite you to join them at a specified date and time. I would advise that this be a private coven ritual, if possible, rather than a public one. This will allow you to make the following observations:

Watch how the High Priest and/or High Priestess act when in a leadership role. Observe how they treat junior members and students of the coven, both individually and as a group.

Pay attention to how the coven members treat the leaders and each other. It's fairly easy to determine whether or not the members treat each other with respect and dignity or if there are political machinations afoot.

Try to talk to each member alone for a few minutes if possible. This will help you to determine whether or not you would be comfortable working with that person on a regular basis.

If you feel that you would be comfortable learning from these teachers and working with the members of this coven on a regular basis, do nothing at that time. Remember that you're not the only one doing evaluations at the moment. Each of them are feeling you out and sizing you up as well. Waiting a day or two will give them time to discuss their feelings and impressions, as well as giving you a little time and space to make sure that you're truly interested. Approach the High Priest or High Priestess on another day and let them know how you felt about your experience at their ritual. Ask if they are accepting new members and, if so, what application procedure you would need to follow in order to be considered.

Now the final section of this chapter – the steps are few, but the lesson is very big. It is ritual etiquette. Your actions, and reactions, can greatly affect whether or not you leave a good impression and take away pleasant memories of your experience.

Always ask in advance about what to expect. Will you be allowed or expected to participate fully or do they want guests to simply witness what's happening?

If you have food allergies or don't drink alcohol, explain the situation and ask if you should be prepared for this. You want to be able to quietly pass over problem foods during a simple feast. I guarantee that they don't want anyone dying during ritual. For example, if you're allergic to peanuts, and they're using peanut butter cookies, you need to know this.

Ask in advance about ritual wear – such as whether or not there's a certain color that you should or shouldn't wear. If they practice ritual nudity or clothing is optional, you should know whether or not they expect it of you as a visitor.

Don't offer to help set up or clean up the ritual area. It sounds like common sense, but you'd be surprised at how many visitors make that offer. Ritual items are usually cleansed, consecrated, and attuned to the energies of the coven members and being handled by a visitor may disturb the balance of that energy.

If you're not sure what to do, then just observe quietly. Watch the others for cues on what to do while standing in circle. If they are clapping in time to a drum, it's most likely that you may clap also.

Afterwards, remember to thank the coven leaders and members for the invitation and experience. You should also be prepared to provide feedback or observations if they ask for it. If they don't invite that many visitors, they may want to know how things appear from an outsider's or newcomer's point of view.

Here are just a few examples of things you should **never** do as a ritual guest:

Never carry on a private conversation during ritual – this is distracting and may interfere with others' ability to focus on or hear what's being said by the ritual leaders.

Never bring a beeper or cell phone into circle – a phone ringing or playing a tune will certainly disrupt the flow within the circle and can interfere with any workings being done. Some groups do allow it, however, if they are set on either silent or vibrate mode, so always ask beforehand.

Never leave or enter a cast circle without permission – this is not only distracting for other participants, but may disrupt the integrity of the circle itself. Even with permission, never leave or enter a cast circle until a door has been cut for you by a ritual leader, designated person, or coven member.

Never make comments or ask questions about the proceedings during ritual – save those until afterward – unless it is expressly stated prior to ritual that the leaders are open to this.

If you see or hear things during the ritual that you don't understand, don't be afraid to ask questions afterward. The key is **HOW** you ask them. If you walk up to a random person and say, "I've never heard of (insert questioned action here). Why did you do that?", then you're going to create an immediate defensive stance in the other person and it will most likely cause bad feelings. However, if you were to walk up to that same person and say, "I found (insert questioned action here) quite interesting. I was wondering if you would be willing to explain to me why that was done", then it will likely be met with a very different reaction. Most coven members are more than willing to explain ritual actions to someone who's less experienced in their ways and traditions.

If you do end up working with a coven and later begin to feel that it's not working out or that things are not what you initially thought them to be, you will need to evaluate some of the potential problems and pitfalls that may be at work. If something feels wrong to you – it probably is. That's a sure sign that it's time to hit the road and look for a new magical home.

Made in the USA
Las Vegas, NV
28 September 2021